WHAT IS TIME?

MINDFUL + PRATIQUE JUNIOR YOGA STORYBOOK

–

BOOK 1:
TIME + SELF

WRITTEN BY

ALENA AHRENS
&
LINDSAY LUTERMAN

ISBN: 9798730761568

OUR SENSE OF TIME'S
IMPORTANT
SO WE DON'T GO TOO FAST
OR SLOW.

BUT WHEN IT
COMES TO TIME,
HOW MUCH DO
YOU REALLY KNOW?

IF WE FOCUS ON WHAT'S HAPPENED,
AND WHAT WE CANNOT CONTROL,

12
WE BECOME TRAPPED IN
MEMORIES
INSTEAD OF FOCUSED ON
OUR GOALS.
5
4
10

WHEN WE FOCUS ON THE FUTURE,
ON WHAT HASN'T HAPPENED YET,

WE MAKE UP STORIES IN OUR HEADS
AND CREATE FALSE REGRET.

WHEN WE THINK OF TIME,
WE MUST FOCUS ON THE NOW.

WE CAN ENJOY THIS MOMENT HERE.
IT IS OUR CHOICE TO ALLOW.

WHAT IS TIME?

TIME IS ALWAYS MOVING. IT NEVER STOPS.
WE CAN'T GO BACK AND WE CAN'T PRESS PAUSE. WE
ALSO CAN'T JUMP INTO THE FUTURE AND WE CAN'T
CHANGE THINGS THAT HAVE ALREADY HAPPENED. DO YOU
WANT TO KNOW WHAT WE CAN DO? WE CAN STAY
FOCUSED ON THE PRESENT.
WHAT IS THE PRESENT?
THE PRESENT IS THIS MOMENT RIGHT NOW. WE ARE IN IT.
WE HAVE THE CHOICE TO STAY RIGHT WHERE WE ARE
AND ENJOY IT. IF WE TRY TO CHANGE WHAT'S ALREADY
HAPPENED, WE ARE WASTING OUR BEAUTIFUL TIME
TRYING TO DO SOMETHING THAT ISN'T POSSIBLE.
IF WE TRY TO CONTROL THE FUTURE, WE ARE SPENDING
SO MUCH ENERGY ON SOMETHING THAT HASN'T HAPPENED
YET. IT'S OKAY TO HAVE GOALS THAT YOU WANT TO
REACH, BUT FOCUS ON WHAT YOU CAN DO NOW TO REACH
THEM.
WHAT CAN WE DO TO BE MORE AWARE OF THIS MOMENT
RIGHT NOW?

BODY SCAN MEDITATION

ONE THING WE CAN TRY IS A BODY SCAN.

WHAT IS A BODY SCAN?

WELL, IT IS EXACTLY WHAT IT SOUNDS LIKE. A BODY SCAN IS WHEN WE FOCUS ON EVERY SINGLE PART OF THE BODY ONE AT A TIME AND NOTICE HOW WE ARE FEELING. WE CAN ALSO RELAX THE BODY THIS WAY, AND HELP OUR MINDS TO QUIET DOWN BY FOCUSING ON ONE THING AT A TIME.

LET'S TRY THIS NOW.

13

BODY SCAN MEDITATION

1. BEGIN BY FINDING A COMFORTABLE PLACE TO SIT OR LIE DOWN. TAKE A DEEP BREATH IN AND MAKE YOUR BELLY NICE AND BIG, AND WHEN YOU BREATHE OUT, MAKE YOUR BELLY AS FLAT AS YOU CAN. AGAIN, BREATHE IN, MAKING YOUR BELLY ROUND LIKE A BALLOON, AND BREATHE OUT, PULLING THE BELLY ALL THE WAY BACK IN. TAKE ONE MORE DEEP BREATH, AND THEN LET YOURSELF BREATHE NORMALLY.

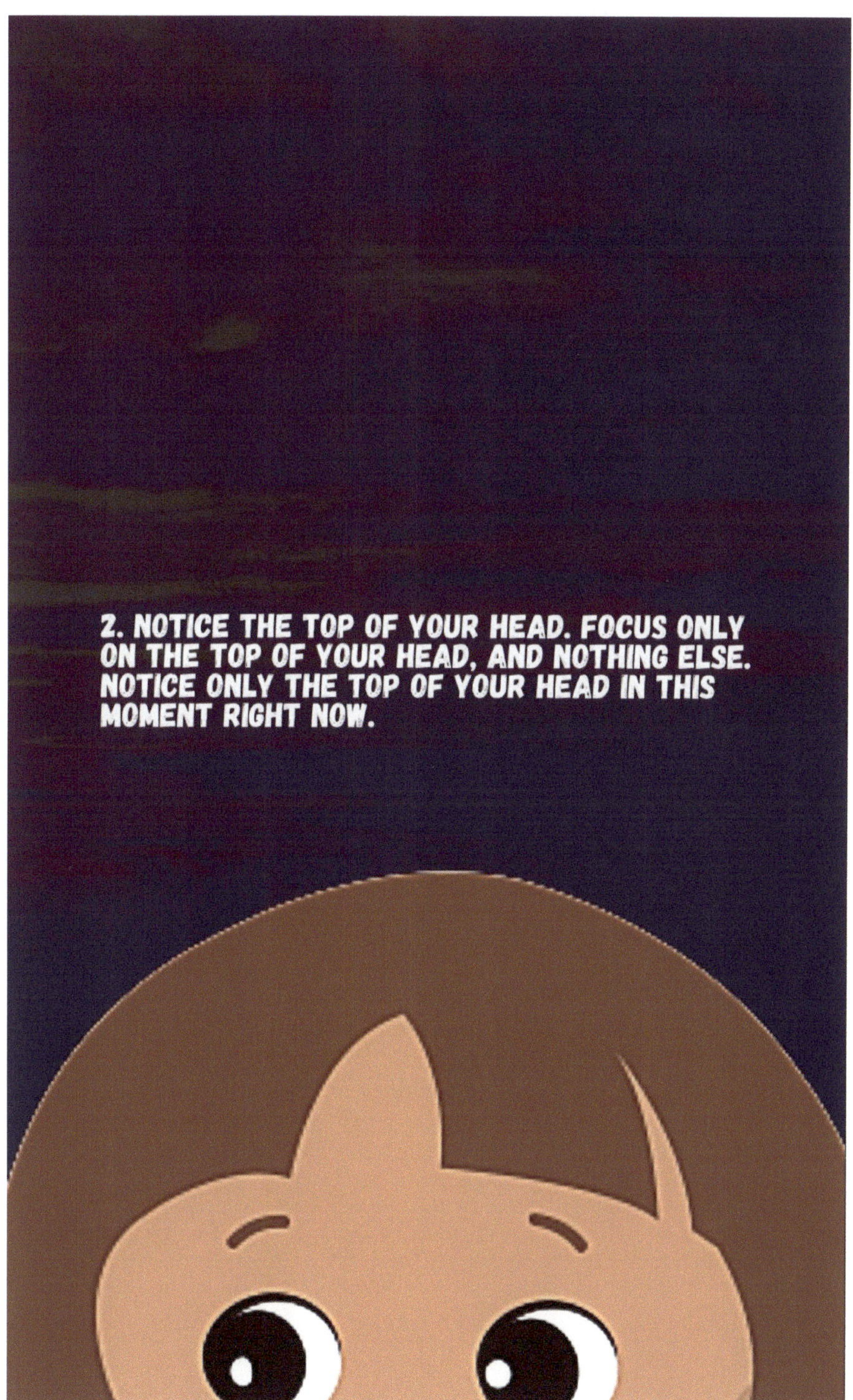

2. NOTICE THE TOP OF YOUR HEAD. FOCUS ONLY ON THE TOP OF YOUR HEAD, AND NOTHING ELSE. NOTICE ONLY THE TOP OF YOUR HEAD IN THIS MOMENT RIGHT NOW.

3. NOW, NOTICE YOUR FOREHEAD. IS IT RELAXED? CAN YOU SOFTEN IT A BIT, ALLOWING YOUR EYEBROWS TO RELAX AS WELL? NOTICE YOUR FOREHEAD AND HOW YOU ARE FEELING.

4. NOW, NOTICE YOUR CHEEKS AND JAW. CAN YOU RELAX THEM BOTH? MAKE SURE YOU AREN'T CLENCHING YOUR JAW. NOTICE HOW THAT FEELS.

5. NOTICE YOUR NOSE AND ONLY YOUR NOSE.
WATCH YOUR BREATHING. IS THE AIR COLD OR
WARM IN YOUR NOSE AS YOU BREATHE IN?
HOW ABOUT WHEN YOU BREATHE OUT?

6. NOTICE YOUR MOUTH NOW. RELAX YOUR LIPS AND MAKE SURE YOUR TEETH ARE NOT CLENCHED TOGETHER. LET YOUR TONGUE RELAX.

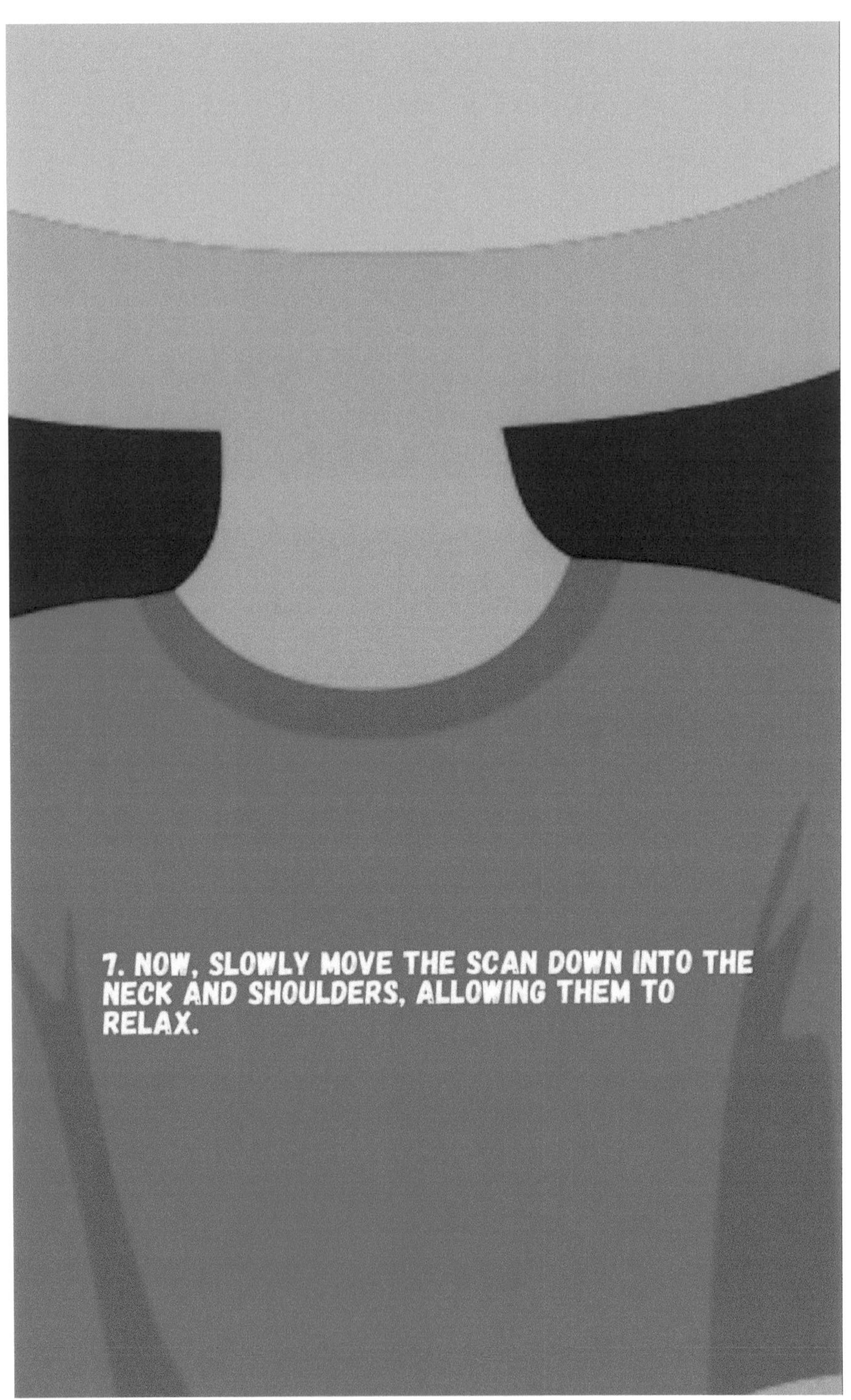

7. NOW, SLOWLY MOVE THE SCAN DOWN INTO THE NECK AND SHOULDERS, ALLOWING THEM TO RELAX.

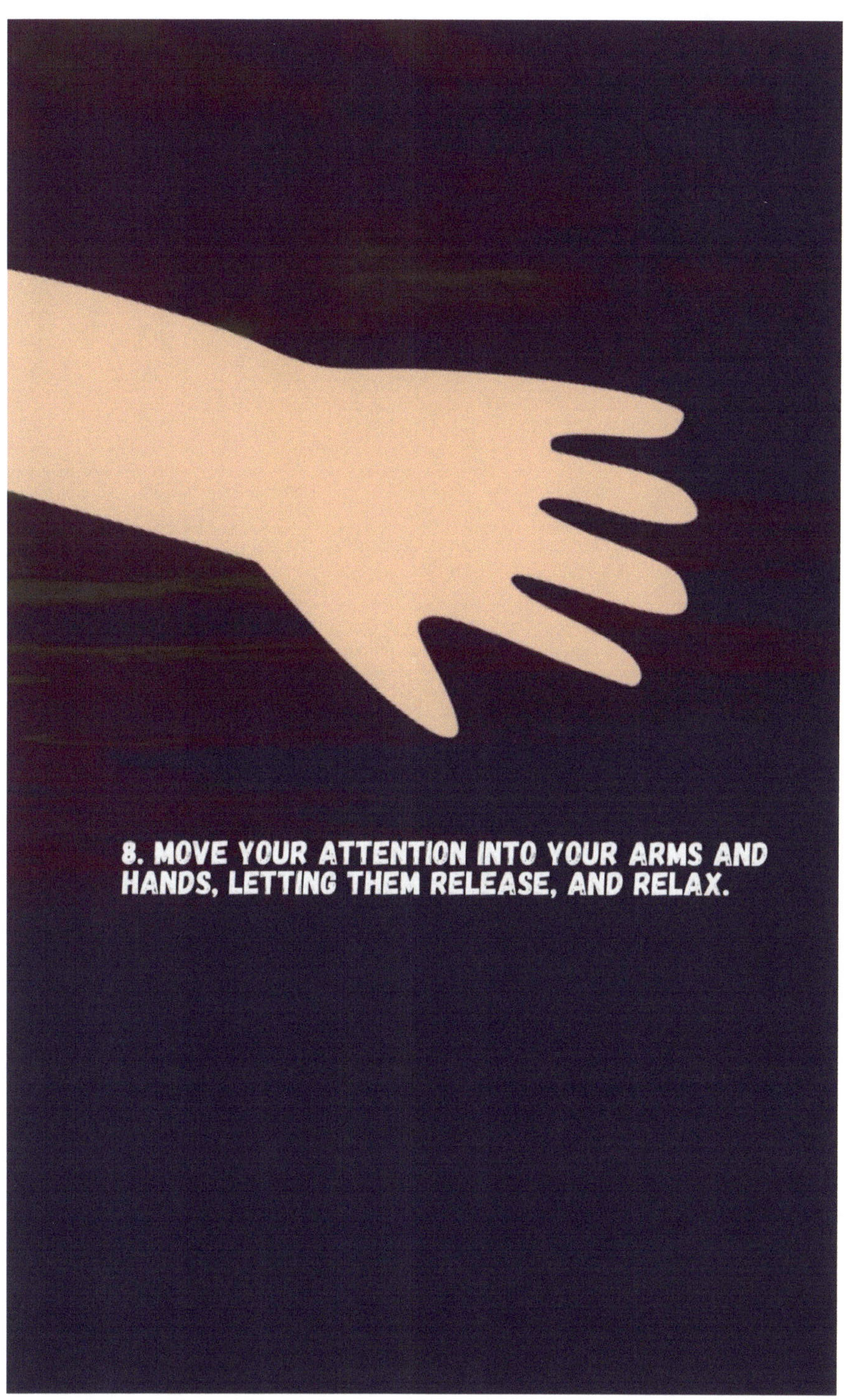

8. MOVE YOUR ATTENTION INTO YOUR ARMS AND HANDS, LETTING THEM RELEASE, AND RELAX.

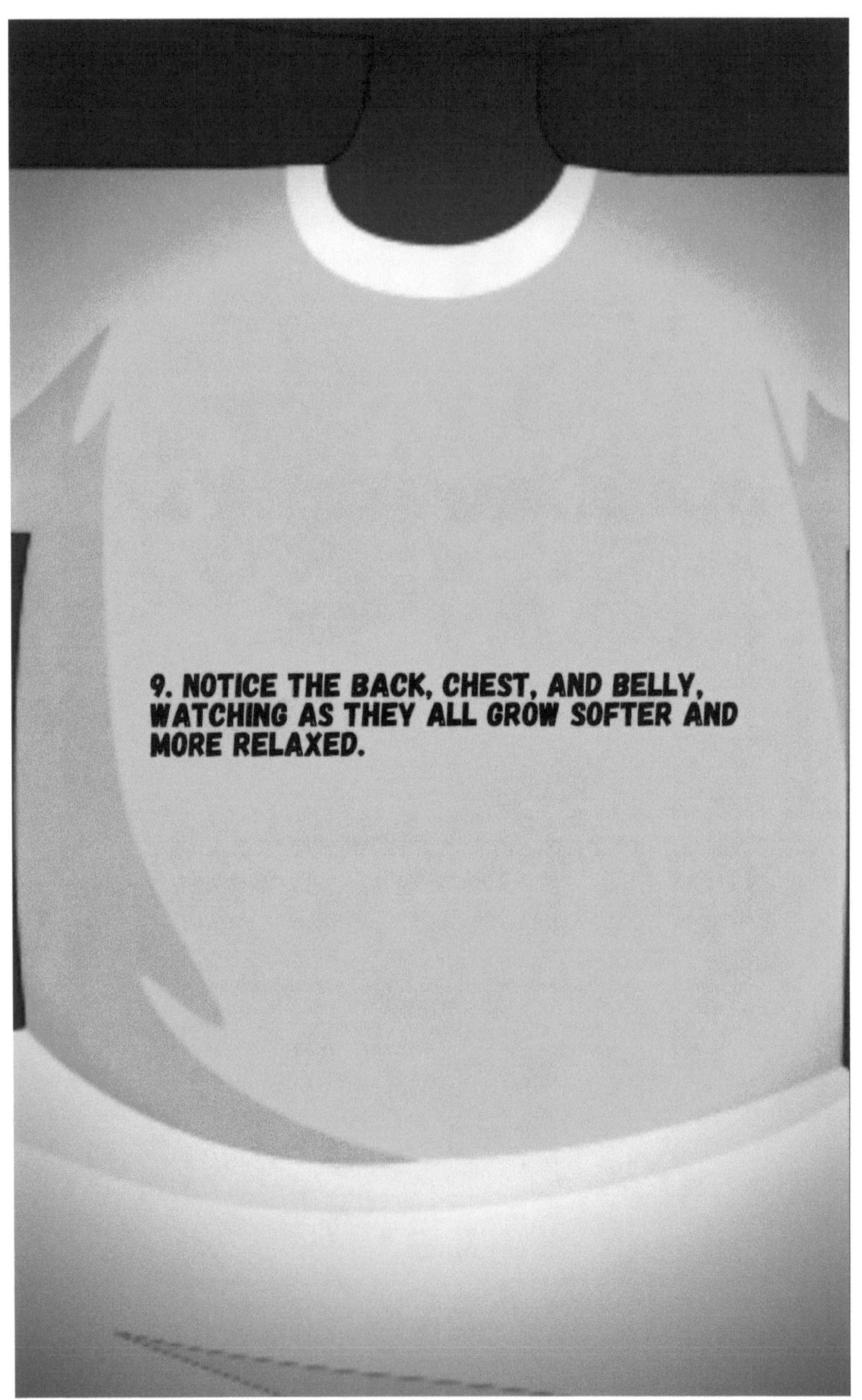

9. NOTICE THE BACK, CHEST, AND BELLY, WATCHING AS THEY ALL GROW SOFTER AND MORE RELAXED.

10. RELAX YOUR HIPS AND DOWN INTO YOUR
LEGS, YOUR FEET, AND FINALLY, YOUR TOES.

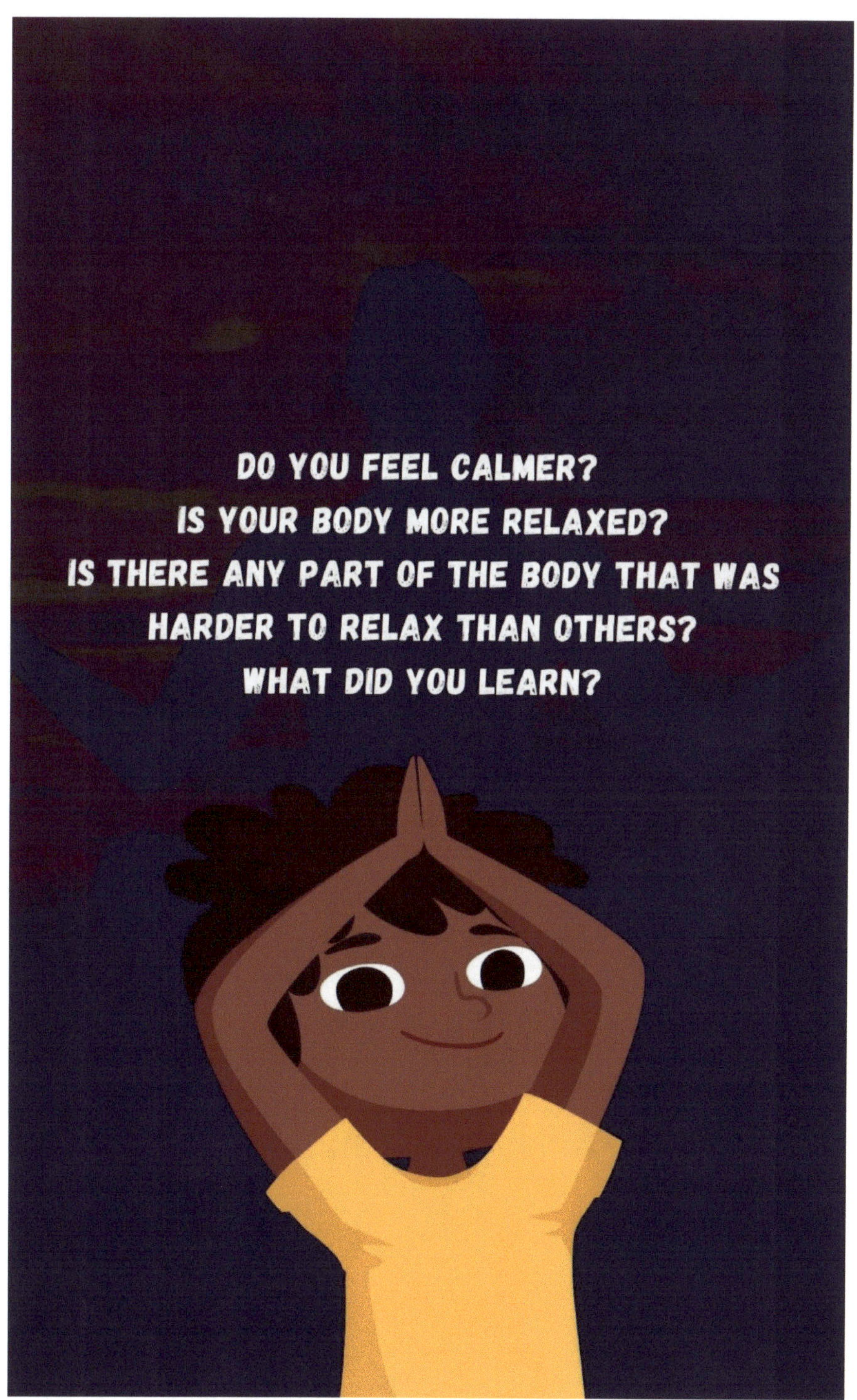

DO YOU FEEL CALMER?
IS YOUR BODY MORE RELAXED?
IS THERE ANY PART OF THE BODY THAT WAS
HARDER TO RELAX THAN OTHERS?
WHAT DID YOU LEARN?

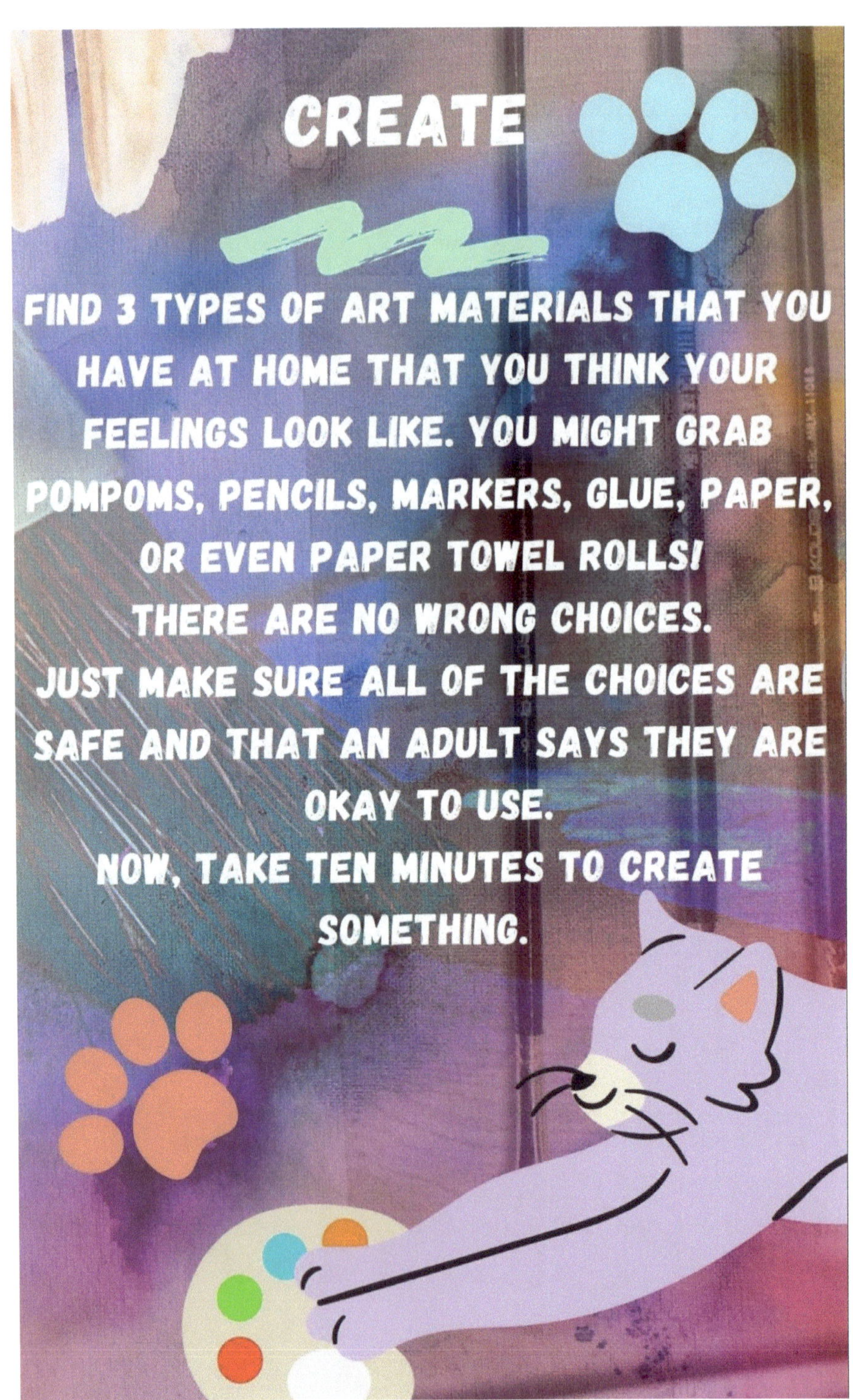

CREATE

FIND 3 TYPES OF ART MATERIALS THAT YOU
HAVE AT HOME THAT YOU THINK YOUR
FEELINGS LOOK LIKE. YOU MIGHT GRAB
POMPOMS, PENCILS, MARKERS, GLUE, PAPER,
OR EVEN PAPER TOWEL ROLLS!
THERE ARE NO WRONG CHOICES.
JUST MAKE SURE ALL OF THE CHOICES ARE
SAFE AND THAT AN ADULT SAYS THEY ARE
OKAY TO USE.
NOW, TAKE TEN MINUTES TO CREATE
SOMETHING.

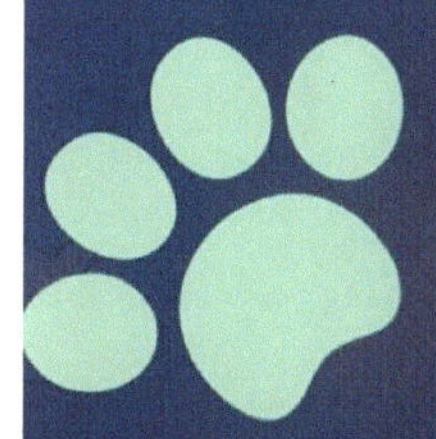

CREATE

WHEN YOU ARE DONE, ANSWER THESE QUESTIONS:

1. WHAT WOULD YOU NAME THIS ARTWORK?
2. WHEN YOU'VE NAMED IT,
3. WHAT MADE YOU DECIDE ON THAT NAME?
4. HOW DOES THIS ART RELATE TO YOUR LIFE?
5. IF THIS ART COULD SPEAK, WHAT PROMISE WOULD IT ASK YOU TO KEEP?
6. DESCRIBE WHAT YOUR ART LOOKS LIKE.
7. WHAT MADE YOU PICK THE MATERIAL YOU USED TO MAKE YOUR ART?
8. WHAT DO YOU THINK ABOUT WHEN YOU LOOK AT YOUR ART?
9. HOW DOES YOUR ART MAKE YOU FEEL?

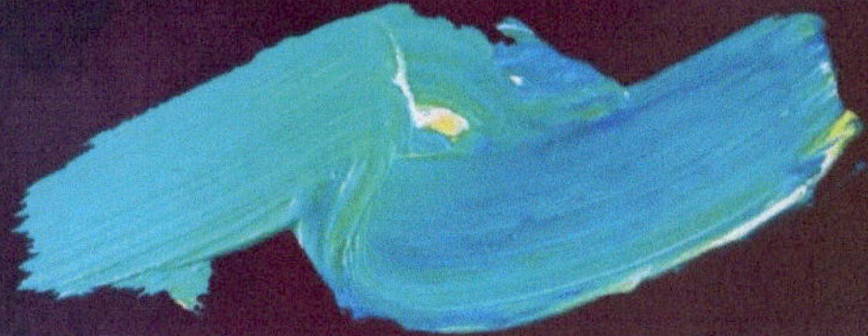

YOGA AND TIME

NOW, LET'S DO SOME YOGA POSES!
PRACTICING YOGA IS A GREAT WAY TO
LEARN MORE ABOUT TIME AND HOW WE
UNDERSTAND IT.
REMEMBER: WHATEVER YOU DO TO ONE
SIDE IN YOGA, MAKE SURE TO DO THE
SAME TO THE OTHER SIDE.

DEEP BREATHING

LET'S START WITH DEEP BREATHING.
THIS IS VERY EASY TO DO.
JUST SIT COMFORTABLY AND FOCUS ON TAKING
DEEP, EVEN, LONG BREATHS.

WARRIOR II

STEP YOUR LEGS OUT WIDE AND POINT ONE FOOT FORWARDS. TURN THE TOES OF YOUR OTHER FOOT SIDEWAYS AND BRING YOUR ARMS OUT TO THE SIDE. LOOK OVER YOUR FRONT HAND.

TREE POSE

STAND ON ONE FOOT AND BRING THE
OTHER FOOT TO YOUR LEG. IMAGINE ROOTS
COMING DOWN THROUGH YOUR FOOT AND
INTO THE GROUND. REACH YOUR ARMS UP
HIGH LIKE BRANCHES.

DANCER'S POSE

LIKE A DANCER, STAND ON ONE FOOT AND
REACH THE OTHER LEG BACK, BENDING
THE KNEE. REACH YOUR HAND BACK FOR
YOUR ANKLE AND BRING YOUR OTHER ARM
OUT IN FRONT OF YOU.

CHILD'S POSE

NOW, START ON YOUR HANDS AND KNEES
AND PRESS YOUR HIPS BACK OVER YOUR
HEELS. STRETCH YOUR ARMS OUT IN FRONT
OF YOU AND BRING YOUR FOREHEAD TO
THE GROUND.
BREATHE DEEPLY AND REST HERE.

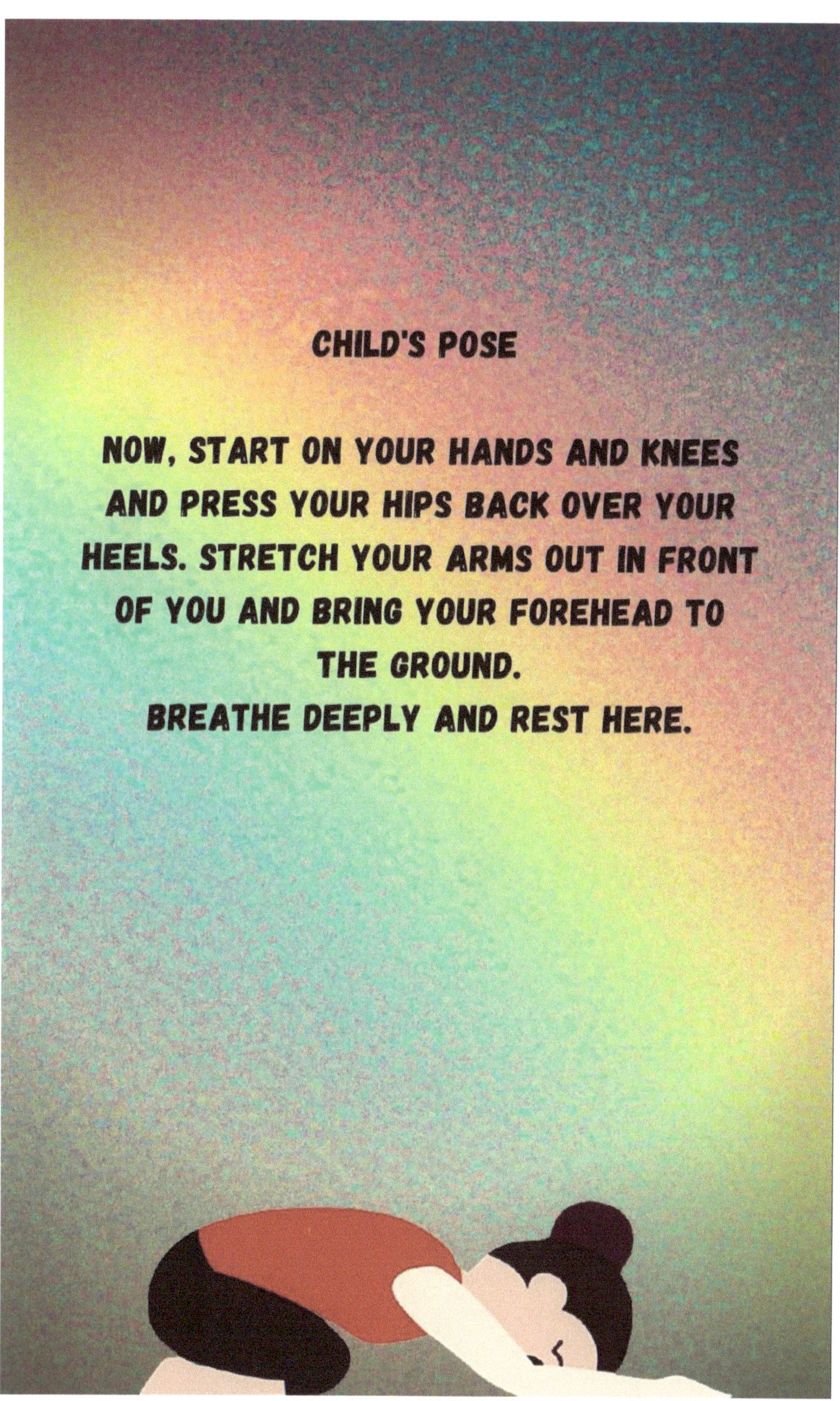

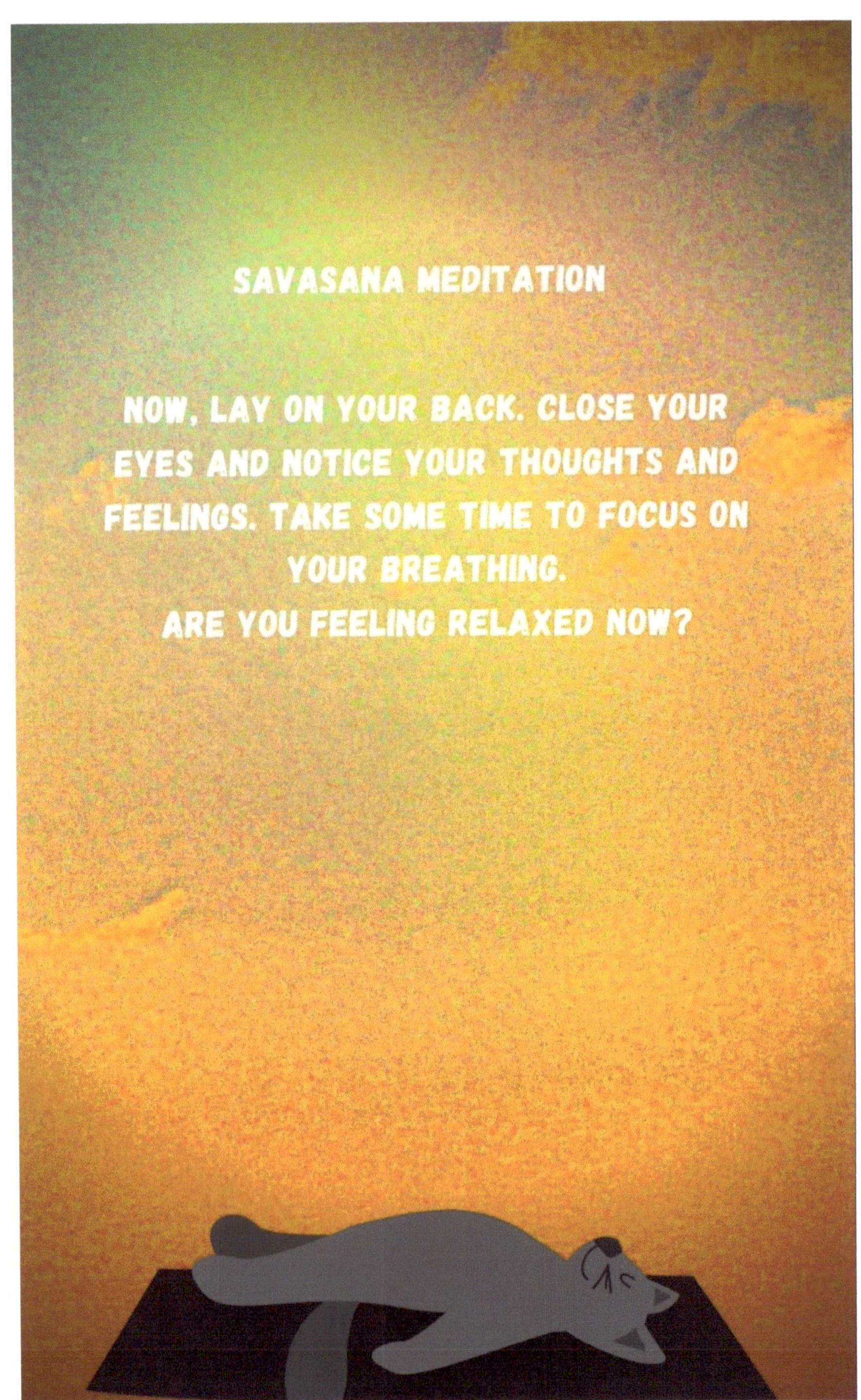

SAVASANA MEDITATION

NOW, LAY ON YOUR BACK. CLOSE YOUR
EYES AND NOTICE YOUR THOUGHTS AND
FEELINGS. TAKE SOME TIME TO FOCUS ON
YOUR BREATHING.
ARE YOU FEELING RELAXED NOW?

ALENA AHRENS IS A CONTEMPORARY AMERICAN–ASIAN ARTIST AND EDUCATOR WHO IS BASED IN THE MIDWEST. HER PASSION FOR EXPLORING THE INTERSECTION OF ART AND WELL–BEING EVOLVED OUT OF SPENDING MUCH OF HER CHILDHOOD IN THAILAND AND HAS LED TO ON–GOING THEORETICAL AND EMPIRICAL RESEARCH IN THE AREAS OF THE ARTS, MINDFULNESS, AND EDUCATIONAL PSYCHOLOGY. SHE EARNED HER MFA IN STUDIO PRACTICES AT THE SCHOOL OF THE ART INSTITUTE OF CHICAGO AND COMPLETED HER PHD IN EDUCATION WITH A FOCUS ON TEACHING AND LEARNING PROCESSES AT THE UNIVERSITY OF MISSOURI ST. LOUIS. SHE ENJOYS DEVELOPING NEW METHODS THAT PROMOTE WELL–BEING BY DRAWING FROM MULTIPLE DOMAINS OF KNOWLEDGE AND OFFERING THEM IN A WORKSHOP FORMAT. ALENA HAS SHARED HER WORK AROUND THE WORLD AND ENJOYS CONNECTING WITH OTHERS THROUGH VIRTUAL PLATFORMS.

LINDSAY LUTERMAN IS AN AUTHOR, YOGA INSTRUCTOR, BLOGGER, AND WELLNESS COACH! ALWAYS A WRITER AT HEART, LINDSAY PUBLISHED HER FIRST BOOK— THE ESCAPE— AT ONLY FIFTEEN YEARS OLD. THAT BOOK SOON BECAME THE FIRST OF A TRILOGY, AND IT ALSO INSPIRED A SPIN-OFF NOVELLA. A FEW YEARS LATER, LINDSAY WROTE AND PUBLISHED HER FIFTH NOVEL— MERCY'S SUNSET. SHE EARNED HER 200 HOUR YOGA TEACHER CERTIFICATION THROUGH THE UNIVERSITY OF MARYLAND CENTER FOR INTEGRATIVE MEDICINE, HER 1000 HOUR YOGA TEACHER CERTIFICATION THROUGH NAROPA UNIVERSITY, AND HER CHILDREN'S YOGA CERTIFICATION. SHE IS MASTERED IN TWO FORMS OF REIKI ENERGY HEALING. SHE HAS ALSO EARNED HER ASSOCIATES OF ARTS IN EARLY CHILDHOOD EDUCATION AND HER BACHELORS OF SCIENCE IN INTERDISCIPLINARY STUDIES— FOCUSSING ON EDUCATION AND HEALTH SCIENCE— THROUGH LIBERTY UNIVERSITY. HER FAVORITE TYPES OF YOGA TO PRACTICE ARE RESTORATIVE AND YIN YOGA.

M + P
jr.